21st Century Skills Library

REAL WORLD MATH: SPORTS

SOCCER

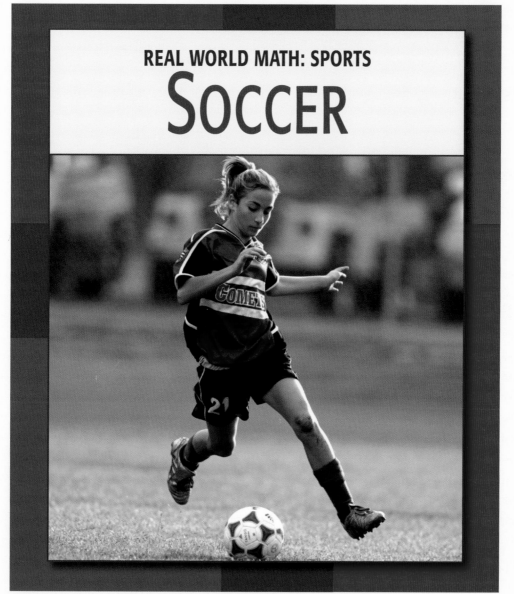

Cecilia Minden and Katie Marsico

Cherry Lake Publishing

Ann Arbor, Michigan

Published in the United States of America by Cherry Lake Publishing
Ann Arbor, Michigan
www.cherrylakepublishing.com

Math Adviser: Tonya Walker, MA, Boston University

Content Adviser: Thomas Sawyer, EdD, Professor of Recreation and Sport Management, Indiana State University

Photo Credits: Cover and pages 1 and 7, ©Shawn Pecor, used under license from Shutterstock, Inc.; page 4, ©ArtmannWitte, used under license from Shutterstock, Inc.; page 8, ©Mike Flippo, used under license from Shutterstock, Inc.; page 10, ©AKV, used under license from Shutterstock, Inc.; page 12, ©iStockphoto.com/amysuem; page 14, ©AP Photo/Hans Pennink; page 17, ©AP Photo/John T. Greilick; page 18, ©AP Photo/ Victor R. Caivano; page 20, ©AP Photo Michel Euler; page 23, ©AP Photo/Shizuo Kambayashi; page 25, ©Lorraine Swanson, used under license from Shutterstock, Inc.; page 26, ©iStockphoto.com/miflippo

Library of Congress Cataloging-in-Publication Data
Minden, Cecilia.
Soccer / by Cecilia Minden and Katie Marsico.
   p. cm.—(Real world math)
Includes bibliographical references and index.
ISBN-13: 978-1-60279-244-9
ISBN-10: 1-60279-244-5
1. Soccer—Juvenile literature. 2. Arithmetic—Problems, exercises,
etc.—Juvenile literature. I. Marsico, Katie, 1980– II. Title. III. Series.
GV943.25.M56 2009
796.334—dc22   2008001401

*Cherry Lake Publishing would like to acknowledge the work of
The Partnership for 21st Century Skills.
Please visit* www.21stcenturyskills.org *for more information.*

TABLE OF CONTENTS

GO FOR THE GOAL!

Soccer is one of the most exciting sports in the world.

You race with your team down the field. You move quickly to reach the ball and kick it to your teammate. Your teammate moves the ball down toward the **opponents'** goal. The goalie braces for the kick. At the last second, the ball is passed back to you. With your final kick, the ball speeds past the goalie and into the net. Score!

Soccer is the most popular sport in the world today. It was adapted from an ancient Chinese game called *tsu chu* (SUU-CHEW). The word *tsu* means "to kick the ball with your feet." The word *chu* means "a ball made of leather." The object of the game was to kick the ball through a hole in a net to score. Like soccer today, players were not allowed to use their hands. It was a very difficult game, and players who were skilled at scoring were celebrated as heroes.

The game of soccer as we know it today began in Great Britain in the 1800s. The name soccer has an interesting history. In the early 1800s, there

REAL WORLD MATH CHALLENGE

Soccer balls come in different sizes. Mary's U6 team (for players 6 years old and younger) uses a size 3 soccer ball. The **circumference** of their ball is 23 inches (58 centimeters), and it weighs 11 ounces (0.31 kilograms). Joe's U10 team uses a size 4 soccer ball. The circumference of their ball is 26 inches (66 cm), and it weighs 13 ounces (0.37 kg). **How much larger is the circumference of the ball used by Joe's team compared to the ball used by Mary's team? How much heavier is the ball used by Joe's team than the ball used by Mary's team? Give your answers in percentages.**

(Turn to page 29 for the answers)

Many people from Europe **immigrated** to the United States in the late 1800s, bringing along their love of the game. Immigrants helped form teams in the towns where they lived. People started forming organized leagues. This led to the formation of the American Soccer League (ASL) in 1921. Today, many Americans enjoy Major League Soccer (MLS), which was formed in 1993.

How do you think the formation of organized teams and leagues helped make the game of soccer more popular?

were two kinds of football: rugby and association football. The Fédération Internationale de Football Association (FIFA) was formed in 1904. FIFA set the rules for rugby and association football. Because "association football" was hard to remember, many people began calling the game "soccer." Today in Europe, many people still refer to soccer as football. The game was firmly established when FIFA became active in Olympic soccer in 1908.

Soccer's biggest **international** competition is the FIFA World Cup. The World Cup began in 1930. Brazil has won five World Cup titles, more than any other team. The U.S. men's team has qualified for,

but never won, the World Cup. The

U.S. women's team, however, has

won the World Cup twice! They

won in 1991 and again in 1999.

Today, the U.S. men's and women's

teams are ranked in the top 20

teams in the world.

Playing soccer takes more than quick feet and coordination. Players also need good math skills.

Soccer is a **competitive** sport,

with very precise rules. Soccer

fields must be a specific size. The

soccer ball can only weigh a certain number of ounces. A limited number

of players are allowed on the field at any single moment. Maybe the most

important numbers are the ones that add up to the winning score!

CHAPTER TWO

A FEW SOCCER BASICS

Goalkeepers are the only players on the field allowed to use their hands.

Soccer is pretty easy to understand. Two teams play against each other.

Each team has a goal. The object of the game is to get the ball into the

opponent's goal. Each team must defend its goal against the opponents.

The team with the highest number of goals at the end of the game wins.

There are 11 players on a soccer team. Ten are field players, and one is the goalkeeper, or goalie.

Field players play one of the following positions:

defender, **midfielder**, or **forward**. Defenders prevent the ball from going into the goal. Midfielders help pass the ball down the field to position it for a goal. Forwards shoot the ball into the goal. The goalkeeper guards the goal from the opposing team.

Field players can't use the area from their shoulders to their fingertips to touch the ball while it is in play. This means they may not use their hands. Only the goalkeeper is allowed to use his hands to stop the ball.

Life & Career Skills

Soccer is one of the purest team sports in the world today. Ask any one of soccer's greats, from Pelé to David Beckham, and they will tell you that a single player cannot win a game for their team. Collaborating with your teammates and creating a game plan result in the best chance for victory.

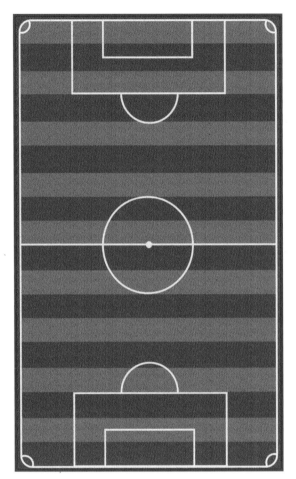

The dimensions of a soccer field will vary depending on the age of the players.

Soccer is a game in which the conditions vary with the age of the players. U8 players have a shorter playing time. They play two 20-minute halves. U17-Adult players have games with two 45-minute halves.

A soccer field must always be longer than it is wide. You can't play soccer on a square field! The lines running along the long sides of the field are called the sidelines. The ball cannot go beyond these lines during a game. The lines running across the short ends of the field are called the end lines. The center circle is in the middle of the field. The

centerline runs through the center circle.

REAL WORLD MATH CHALLENGE

The field size for an international soccer match is 110 to 120 yards (101 to 110 m) x 70 to 80 yards (64 to 73 m). **How many square yards are in a 110 yard x 70 yard field? How many square yards are in a field that measures 120 yards x 80 yards? What is the difference between the two?**

(Turn to page 29 for the answers)

The goals are at either end of the field. They are located in the center

of the end lines. For adults, the official size of the goal is 8 feet (2.4 m) by

24 feet (7.3 m). For the youngest players, the goal size is 4 feet (1.2 m) by

6 feet (1.8 m).

To begin the game, the ball is placed in the center of the center circle

for the kickoff. The two teams are each on their own sides of the field.

Players from both teams work to keep possession of the ball.

The defending team cannot be in the center circle. The **referee** blows the

whistle, and the ball is kicked. The player who first kicked the ball cannot

touch the ball again until another player touches the ball. Each team is

trying to get possession of the ball and score. The teams are also trying

to keep the other team from scoring. Soccer is a fast-moving game with

players racing up and down the field.

There are only four reasons to stop play: a goal is scored, the ball goes out of bounds, a player is injured, or the referee calls a foul. A foul is an illegal play. Referees can give either yellow or red cards, depending on the intensity of the foul. A yellow card is a warning. A red card means the player is out of the game. Players foul by kicking, pushing, or tripping another player. They can also get a foul for handling or holding the ball. There are other fouls, but these are the basics. When a player fouls, the other team gets a free kick.

How is math important to soccer? Field size, soccer ball size, rules, and different methods of scoring are all examples. Another example is how professional players use numbers to rack up impressive records. Let's meet two players who have helped make soccer a popular sport.

CHAPTER THREE

DO THE MATH: IMPRESSIVE PROS

There are great soccer players all over the world. The United States

recognizes outstanding players at the National Soccer Hall of Fame,

located in Oneonta, New York. Since 1950, many gifted soccer players have

been **inducted**. One Hall of Famer is Mia Hamm.

*Mia Hamm speaks at her National Soccer
Hall of Fame induction in 2007.*

Hamm began her amazing career at age 15 when she joined the U.S. Women's National Soccer Team. She was the youngest person ever to join the team. Her first game was against China in 1987. She played her last professional game against Mexico in 2004. During her 17-year career, she racked up some impressive stats.

Hamm graduated from the University of North Carolina (UNC) in 1994. She led her team to four National Collegiate Athletic Association (NCAA) championships. When she graduated, she held the all-time record for most conference goals—103! Hamm continued to play with the U.S. Women's National Soccer Team. She was a key player in the World Cup victories in 1991 and 1999. She also helped her team win Olympic gold medals in 1996 and 2004. Between 1987 and 2004, Hamm played an impressive 275 international games.

FIFA honored Hamm with the Women's World Player of the Year award in both 2001 and 2002. In 2004, FIFA created a list of the 125 greatest living soccer players. They named only two women: Hamm and Michelle Akers. They were also the only Americans listed. For five years in a row (1994–1998), Hamm was the U.S. Soccer Federation Female Athlete of the Year. She was elected to the Soccer Hall of Fame in 2007.

REAL WORLD MATH CHALLENGE

Hamm played soccer at UNC for four years. During that time, she made 103 conference goals. **What was the average number of goals she scored each year?**

(Turn to page 29 for the answer)

Perhaps the most famous soccer player of all time was inducted into the Hall of Fame in 1993. Edson Arantes do Nascimento was born in 1940 in Brazil. Most people know him as Pelé (PAY-lay). As a child, Pelé was very poor. He shined shoes

to help support his family.

His father, a former soccer

player, taught him how to

play the game. A famous

soccer player from Brazil,

Waldemar de Brito (wal-

DAY-mar DAY BREE-toh),

saw Pelé play. He was very

impressed. He told people

that Pelé would be "the

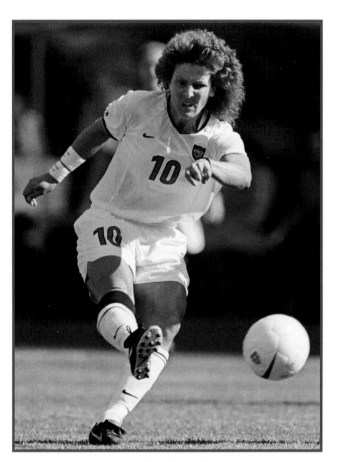

*Michelle Akers shoots
the ball during a match
against China in 1999.*

greatest soccer player in the world." Pelé began playing with a team from

the town of Santos. He scored a goal in his very first game.

Pelé holds the Olympic torch in 2004.

In 1958, Pelé scored six goals to help Brazil's National team win its first World Cup. He was only 17 years old. In 1970, he helped Brazil win another World Cup. It was a 4–1 win over Italy. Pelé was proud because he made Brazil's 100th World Cup goal. During his career, he played 1,360 games and made 1,280 goals.

REAL WORLD MATH CHALLENGE

During his career, Pelé scored 1,280 goals. Another player from Brazil is reported to have scored 1,329 goals. **How many more goals did he score than Pelé?**

(Turn to page 29 for the answer)

In 1974, he left the Santos team. Two years later, Pelé came out of retirement to join the Cosmos of the North American Soccer League. He played with them for two years. Many credit Pelé with making soccer a popular sport in the United States. Soon other international players began playing for U.S. teams.

Pelé and Hamm both used numbers to rack up amazing scores and career victories. Many other players and teams also hold impressive records. Let's read about how they use math to create winning numbers.

CHAPTER FOUR

DO THE MATH: REMARKABLE SOCCER RECORDS

Ronaldo dribbles the ball during a World Cup match against Chile in 1998.

Pelé referred to fellow Brazilian Ronaldo Luis Nazário de Lima as "one of the greatest." Ronaldo and his team won the World Cup in 1994 and in 2002. He was named FIFA Player of the Year three times (1996, 1997, and

2002). He is the all-time World Cup goal scorer, with 15 goals in 19 games in three World Cups.

Hall of Famer Mia Hamm wasn't the first woman to be elected to the National Soccer Hall of Fame. April Heinrichs was elected in 1998. She was a captain of the 1991 World Cup championship team. In 1986 and 1989, Heinrichs was named U.S. Soccer Female Athlete of the Year. She went from player to head coach of the U.S. Women's National Soccer Team from 2000 to 2005.

Landon Donovan is another player with an impressive record. He is a member of the LA Galaxy professional soccer team. He is also a member of the U.S. Men's National Soccer Team. He scored a goal in his very first international game in October 2000. Only six other people have done that! Donovan was named U.S. Soccer Athlete of the Year in 2003 and 2004.

He led the national team in points for three years in a row. During the 2006 World Cup, he played in 16 of the 18 matches and scored 6 goals.

A young woman player to watch is Marta Vieira da Silva. She is considered to be one of the best women soccer players today. At 5 feet 4 inches (1.6 m) tall, she is a force on the field. Marta was a member of Brazil's team at the 2004 Olympics. They won the silver medal. She was named the FIFA Woman's World Player of the Year in 2006 and 2007.

REAL WORLD MATH CHALLENGE

Ronaldo Luis Nazário de Lima scored 15 goals in 19 games during 3 World Cup competitions. **What was the average number of goals he scored per game during those competitions? What was the average number of goals he scored in the 3 World Cup competitions?**

(Turn to page 29 for the answers)

Marta Vieira da Silva plays in a match against Japan in 2007.

Brazilian soccer player Ronaldo Luis Nazário de Lima worked hard to achieve success as a professional soccer player. It would be easy for him to just sit back and enjoy the fame that comes with being one of the best soccer players in the world. But he remembers how soccer brought him from the poverty of his childhood to where he is today. He gives back to the world community by volunteering for the United Nations Development Programme (UNDP). As a UNDP goodwill ambassador, he works to help bring education and sports to **refugee** children around the world. He once said in an interview, "All children deserve the same opportunity to play and a chance for a better future."

Players could not set records without the help of their entire team. Teams can hold records, too. Brazil holds the record as the only country to play in every World Cup. Italy has won four World Cups, and Germany has won three.

You don't have to play in the World Cup to be competitive. Each week, there are thousands of soccer games being played all over the globe. Each game is important to both players and fans. All of those players need numbers to keep track of just how well they—and their teams—are doing!

CHAPTER FIVE

GET YOUR GAME GOING!

Many young soccer players compete in local leagues and on school teams.

There are many ways to get your own soccer game going. Many kids

play soccer at their school during recess. There are also organized leagues.

The American Youth Soccer Organization (AYSO) was formed in 1964 in

California. Players' ages are between 4 and 18. There are AYSO programs

Cleats, shin guards, and a ball are the basic equipment you need to play soccer.

in the United States, the U.S. Virgin Islands, and Trinidad and Tobago. You can find other teams with the Boys and Girls Clubs of America, the YMCA, and city leagues. Many parents support their kids' teams by attending games.

It is also fun to get a game going with your friends. All you need is a soccer ball, but some other things will help keep you safe and comfortable. Soccer players generally wear shorts and a loose-fitting short-sleeved shirt. This keeps them cool and doesn't restrict their movements.

Shin guards are required during organized competitions. Shin guards are sturdy plastic shields that strap to the lower part of your legs. You pull your soccer socks over the shin guards to help hold them in place. Shin guards help keep your legs from getting bruised. Soccer players also wear cleats. Cleats have hard knobs on the bottom to give players traction to avoid sliding on the grass and into other players.

21st Century Content

Having fun while playing soccer also means playing it safe. Make sure you keep your health and safety in mind when you get a game going with your friends. Drink plenty of water, especially if it is very warm outside, to stay **hydrated**. If a ball bounces into the street, make sure you and your friends look before crossing to retrieve the ball. And be sure to have extra Band-Aids for cuts and injuries. Can you think of some other health and safety tips for soccer players?

REAL WORLD MATH CHALLENGE

There are some 650,000 players in AYSO. Girls make up 40 percent of these players. **What percentage of the players are boys? Based on the total number of players (650,000), how many girls play in the AYSO? How many boys play in the AYSO?**

(Turn to page 29 for the answers)

You've seen basketball players dribble the ball down the center court. Soccer players also dribble the ball, but they use their feet. Short taps on the ball make it possible for players to run with the ball and still have control. You need hours of practice to become good at dribbling. Eventually, you will become skilled at using your feet, thighs, and even your head to keep the ball moving.

Soccer is a team sport. One person may kick the ball into the goal, but it takes all the other players to help get the ball to the scoring position. Playing with friends is the best way to practice passing the ball back and forth.

An official adult soccer game lasts 90 minutes. The average adult soccer player runs about 7 miles (11.3 kilometers) during that time! You won't need to travel quite that far, but soccer will keep you moving—you can count on it!

REAL WORLD MATH CHALLENGE ANSWERS

Chapter One

Page 5

The difference in circumferences between the 2 balls is 3 inches.

26 inches − 23 inches = 3 inches

This means that the soccer ball used by Joe's team is 13 percent larger than the ball used by Mary's team.

3 inches ÷ 23 inches = 0.13 = 13%

The difference in weights between the 2 balls is 2 ounces.

13 ounces − 11 ounces = 2 ounces

This means that the soccer ball used by Joe's team is 18 percent heavier than the ball used by Mary's team.

2 ounces ÷ 11 ounces = 0.18 = 18%

Chapter Two

Page 11

There are 7,700 square yards (7,041 m) in a 110 yard x 70 yard field.

110 yards x 70 yards = 7,700 square yards

There are 9,600 square yards (8,778 m) in a 120 yard x 80 yard field.

120 yards x 80 yards = 9,600 square yards

The difference between the two fields is 1,900 square yards (1,737 m).

9,600 square yards − 7,700 square yards = 1,900 square yards = 1,900 square yards

Chapter Three

Page 16

Hamm averaged 25.75 conference goals each year at UNC.

103 goals ÷ 4 years = 25.75 goals

Page 18

The other player scored 49 more goals than Pelé.

1,329 goals − 1,280 goals = 49 goals

Chapter Four

Page 22

Ronaldo Luis Nazário de Lima scored an average of 0.79 goals per game.

15 goals ÷ 19 games = 0.79 goals per game

He scored an average of 5 goals per World Cup competition.

15 goals ÷ 3 World Cups = 5 goals per World Cup

Chapter Five

Page 27

Boys make up 60 percent of the players in the AYSO.

100 percent − 40 percent = 60 percent

There are 260,000 girls in the AYSO.

650,000 players x 0.40 = 260,000 girls

There are 390,000 boys in the AYSO.

650,000 players x 0.60 = 390,000 boys

Glossary

circumference (sur-KUHM-fur-uhnss) the distance around an object such as a soccer ball

competitive (kuhm-PET-uh-tiv) the efforts of two or more parties to win a sporting event

defender (di-FEND-ur) a field player who protects the goal

forward (FOR-wurd) a player who makes many shots on goal during a soccer game

hydrated (HY-dray-tid) has the right amount of fluid

immigrated (IM-uh-grayt-id) moved from one country to another

inducted (in-DUHK-tid) admitted as a new member

international (in-tur-NASH-uh-nuhl) worldwide, or global

midfielder (MID-feeld-ur) a player who links the offense and defense

opponents (uh-POH-nuhnts) players on the other side or opposite team

referee (ref-uh-REE) a game official

refugee (REF-yuh-jee) a person forced to leave home because of a war, natural disaster, or some other event

FOR MORE INFORMATION

Books

Buckley, James. *Soccer Superstars*. Mankato, MN: Child's World, 2007.

Dorling Kindersley Publishing (staff). *Eyewitness Books: Soccer*. New York: DK Publications, 2005.

Web Sites

Major League Soccer
web.mlsnet.com/index.jsp
Get scores and news from Major League Soccer

National Soccer Hall of Fame: Games
www.soccerhall.org/games.htm
Play online soccer games

Official Web Site of U.S. Soccer
www.ussoccer.com/
Learn about the U.S. Men's and Women's national teams

INDEX

ABOUT THE AUTHORS

Cecilia Minden, PhD, is a former classroom teacher and university professor. She now enjoys being a literacy consultant and author of children's books. She lives with her family near Chapel Hill, North Carolina. She would like to thank all her soccer-playing nieces and nephews for helping her to enjoy "the beautiful game."

Katie Marsico worked as a managing editor in children's publishing before becoming a freelance writer. She lives near Chicago, Illinois, with her husband and two children. She dedicates this book to her daughter and future soccer champion, Maria A. Marsico.

WITHDRAWN